Me and Waffle

Me and Waffle

SARAH KHANZADEH

StoryTerrace

Text Sarah Khanzadeh
Copyright © Sarah Khanzadeh and StoryTerrace
Text is private and confidential

First print December 2022

StoryTerrace
www.StoryTerrace.com

We would like to dedicate this book to the incredible charity, Hearing Dogs for Deaf People, which has helped change so many lives and to all the awesome volunteers that help create partnerships just like Sarah & Waffle.

Forever Thankful

CONTENTS

SARAH'S BIRTH AND EARLY YEARS	9
SARAH'S SCHOOL DAYS	17
THE ARRIVAL OF WAFFLE IN OUR LIVES AND THE HUGE DIFFERENCE SHE MADE	23
WAFFLE AND SARAH'S ADVENTURES TOGETHER	41
ALL THE FUN OF CRUFTS	55
LOOKING FORWARD TO THE FUTURE WITH CONFIDENCE	67
MORE ABOUT HEARING DOGS	75
SARAH AND SAPEDEH IN THEIR OWN WORDS	85

SARAH'S BIRTH AND EARLY YEARS

Sarah was born in 2003 when we were living in Uxbridge, to me, Sapedeh, and my husband Majid, our first and only child. She was born a week prematurely in the early baby unit and difficulties during the birth meant she had to be on oxygen for a couple of weeks afterwards at Wrexham Park Hospital.

Her arrival should have been such a joyful time for us, as it should be for any new parents – instead, we just felt scared. It was only much later that we would learn that Sarah had been born with Cytomegalovirus (CMV) infection – a virus that transfers from a mother to her baby with no symptoms at all during the pregnancy. Sarah had a very small head when she was born and would also go on to develop a hearing loss, although we knew nothing of this when we first laid eyes on her.

At the time, although we were overjoyed at her arrival, and we stared at her in wonder as all new parents gaze at their new arrival, I simply didn't know why my new baby wasn't healthy. Her eventual diagnosis would be shocking and devastating news, although it meant that, if nothing else, we did at least have a name for what was wrong.

But for a whole, seemingly interminable month after the birth, I was in hospital not knowing what was wrong with my precious new daughter – and no one was able to tell me.

These days, there is a test for CMV which is available seven or eight months into the pregnancy, but unfortunately that wasn't available when Sarah arrived, and the CMV wasn't picked up in my case while I was expecting her.

It seemed that we were facing a pretty uncertain future, and I felt very much as though I was on my own, with very little in the way of support. It was exciting and a joy to bring Sarah home where we wanted her to be at long last, but I also felt extremely apprehensive. Most of my own family was back in Iran, even though I'd lived in the UK since my father came to do a PhD at Brunel University decades before, and so it felt as though I didn't have too much back-up to help me. We were going through a real rollercoaster of emotions, with so many highs and lows, and it was very hard to enjoy our baby in the usual way, as we should have been doing, even though of course we loved her very much.

The health visitor noticed that Sarah wasn't making her milestones and that the development you'd expect to see in a baby her age was delayed. It was only when my daughter was around six months old that we got an appointment at the Child Development Centre (CDC) Hillingdon at Uxbridge. An MRI scan confirmed white spots of calcification on the brain, and that was when we were first told about CMV. Sarah had a blood test which showed a positive result for the virus.

It was around then that I really started questioning everything. It felt as though the world had come to a complete stop. I didn't feel I had enough information, but what I did have I wasn't really processing properly because of the shock. Essentially, however, we were told Sarah would need to be monitored until we really understood what the implications of CMV would be likely to be for her and her future.

Then, when Sarah was around eight or nine months old, we began to realise that she wasn't responding to some ordinary sounds in the way you'd expect. Our GP referred us to the audiology department at Hillingdon Hospital. The long waiting lists meant that she was just a month shy of her second birthday before we got an appointment, at which she was diagnosed as being profoundly deaf. It was like something from your very worst nightmare. I felt anxious about what this would mean, and what the future held for my daughter. Would she spend her life in a silent world?

Sarah had passed all her newborn hearing tests, after all, so we hadn't realised it would be an issue. But then she lost nearly her entire ability to hear during her first six or seven months of life, as the CMV virus made its presence felt in her body.

And, of course, the moment Sarah's deafness was diagnosed, we were keen to understand what had caused it. The consultant from a local hospital sent us off for some tests, which all came back clear initially. But I kept on digging, as this still didn't feel right to me – and I think I was born a fighter!

So I filled in a form and requested all of Sarah's medical notes from birth from the hospital where my daughter was born. When they arrived some 10 days later, I sat down and went through them all page by page.

While I was doing this, I came across a blood test for CMV which was positive. This had been done when Sarah was still a newborn baby. Yet I didn't recall anyone telling me about any positive test results at the time. Yet there it was in black and white in front of me.

I had no idea what the letters CMV even stood for at that point, never mind what it was, and so I started to do more research myself. That's how I learned about the condition and the devastating effects it can have on a newborn baby.

Then I learned I could (and should) have been given an option for Sarah to have anti-viral drugs. But the hospital had not offered this to us on the day of her birth – indeed, they hadn't even discussed the positive test result with us.

I learned all this once Sarah turned two. The cause of her deafness was infection, CMV infection.

At the time, I was living a three-minute drive away from my local hospital. But I chose to go to another hospital in a different borough as I thought the care would be better there. Sadly, I could not have been more wrong!

So really we've been through the whole range of emotions. And, even now, 18 years on, whenever I think about what we went through, it still has the power to bring tears to my eyes.

It's not something I have even been able to get over, and, to be honest, I am not sure I ever will, no matter how much time passes.

As for her hearing loss, Sarah had two hearing aids fitted, and wore dummy ones first of all, just to get used to having something behind her ears.

But while she coped reasonably well with hearing aids, I knew that was Sarah really needed was cochlear implants. She was three when she had the first one fitted surgically at the ENT hospital in London's Kings Cross.

The results were swift – within months of the operation, she slowly started making speech sounds rather than merely babbling. (Her speech had also been pretty delayed.) But I knew she would benefit significantly from having a second implant, and so I fought for that – Sarah had the second cochlear implant fitted when she was four. Typically, however for funding reasons, the NHS only fits one. But I believe I was right to insist on them both being fitted before she started at school proper, to give her education the very best chance.

Not every deaf child is able to have two implants fitted – so it's a good job I was born a fighter!

There were around 14 months between operations, and as mentioned I really had to battle the NHS locally for the second implant, which was fitted at the same hospital. I argued in court that without implants in both ears, Sarah would not know where sound was coming from, and I believe I was right to take on and win that battle. I have no idea how other parents in a similar situation would fare if they were not prepared to dig their heels in.

The good news was that Sarah's speech began to improve steadily, helped along with some sessions we had with a very good speech therapist.

But really the journey with her deafness and CMV had only just begun. We had no idea at all of what lay ahead.

What is a cochlear implant?

Cochlear implants provide a sensation of hearing to those with permanent, severe-to-profound deafness, and who cannot hear the full range of speech sounds with standard hearing aids.

An implant has two parts: one is worn like a hearing aid, behind the ear or clipped on to clothing, while the other is surgically implanted.

The implant itself turns sound into electrical signals. Instead of simply making sounds louder, like a conventional hearing aid does, it provides a sensation of hearing by directly stimulating the auditory nerve using electrical signals.

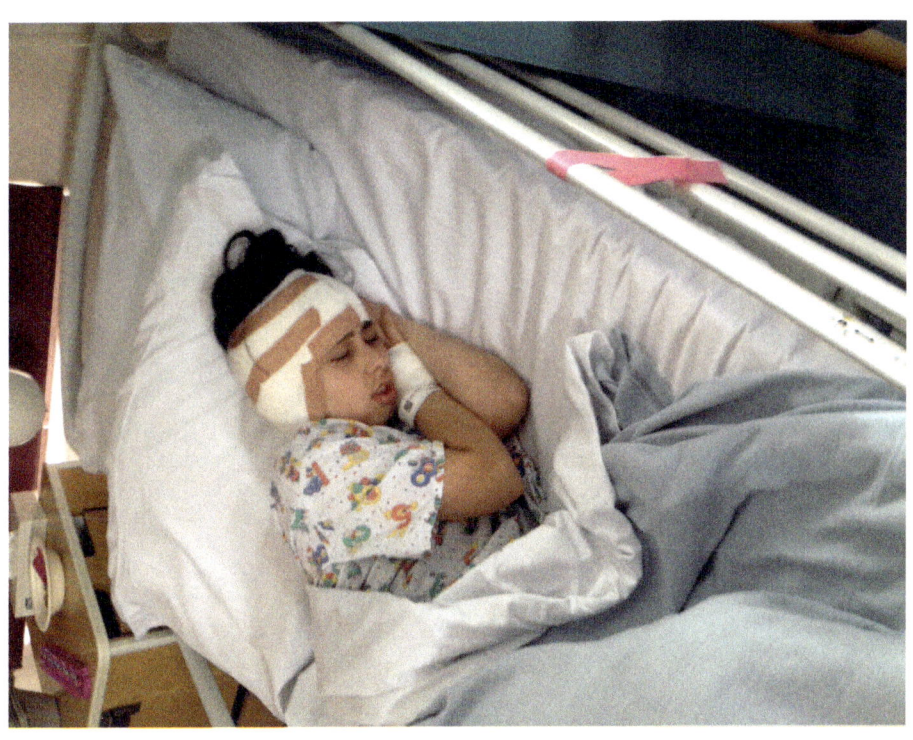

Sarah's first cochlear implant surgery

SARAH'S SCHOOL DAYS

Before we knew it, it was time for Sarah to start at nursery, which, like most kids, she did initially part-time to get used to it. It was a big milestone for her, as it is for any child. And as her parents, we were filled with trepidation, as any mum and dad would be.

She went to one locally at Glebe Primary School, and this was a mainstream nursery with a hearing-impaired unit attached to it. Her needs, such as speech therapy, had already been outlined in what is known as an EHCP or Educational Healthcare Plan.

Sapedeh remembers vividly that, like any parent, she was incredibly nervous for Sarah when she went to nursery for the first time, and it was a real wrench leaving her behind on that first day. Thankfully, though, Sarah adapted pretty quickly and well to her cochlear implants and was keeping them in place and turned on all the time she was awake, even though they were quite chunky and cumbersome objects back in those days, and she was still quite new to having them when she started at nursery. Of course, she found every day exhausting, as most deaf children do – after all, it can be easy to forget that they have to work and concentrate so much harder to take in the same information at the same rate as their hearing peers.

Equally, no other children at the nursery signed. By then Sarah was using sign language and gestures, but other children were hearing and so, unsurprisingly, had no idea about sign language or how it could be used to communicate.

The months raced past and soon it was time to say goodbye to the nursery. We could hardly believe it, but Sarah was setting off for her first day at primary school. Again, as I waved goodbye to her at the school gates on her first day, it was hard. But I had more reason than most mums to be concerned, and these weren't the first-day nerves of any parent. Sarah really struggled to fit in with her peers and a lack of speech made communication, and therefore socialising with the other kids, a real challenge for her – making friends seemed to come so much more easily to the other kids. It was heartbreaking that she never came home to tell us about who she'd spoken to that day, or with birthday party invitations, and she never asked if she could bring a pal home for tea.

By now her contemporaries, all aged around five or six, were able to speak quite well, but Sarah did not really have the language tools needed to have a meaningful conversation with someone else. She was dealing with an awful lot more than her classmates, and so it was that much harder for her to form friendships in quite the same way as they did.

There was on particular teacher, however, a Miss Mac, who was herself deaf in one ear, and so she understood what life can be like when you can't hear well. She helped Sarah, for example, one day after some other kids had been mean to her.

"Ignore them," she whispered in Sarah's ear as she crouched down next to her after she'd noticed Sarah sitting by herself one break time. "Just go out into the playground with the others and don't take any notice."

Sarah did exactly as she was encouraged. And, after that, any time Sarah felt nervous, she would just go straight to Miss Mac for help.

You should never underestimate the impact a single person can have on someone's experiences, especially those of a young person and particularly a teacher; Sarah was a much happier little girl thanks to the dedicated support of Miss Mac.

When it came time for her to make the move to secondary school, Sarah was understandably quite nervous, not least because it meant a significant change in routine. Of course, it is always quite a big transition for any child to make, but it was one that was so much more challenging for Sarah to go through. At Vyners School, Ickenham, again she attended mainstream classes and there was a hearing-impaired unit there.

I'll be honest, at first she really struggled. After her first day, she came home and I could see that she looked upset.

"What's the matter?" I asked.

"I hate it there, Mum. I'm not going back to Vyners! I don't know anyone there. No one is talking to me and I don't know how anything works or where I have to be."

It was clearly an alien environment to her. So on Sarah's second day at the school, I took her in myself and had a chat with staff at the hearing-impaired unit. Thankfully they were really supportive, and said she could go and sit in the unit any time she wanted to – she ended up spending a lot of the school day there.

But while this was great, and very helpful in making her feel calm and included, it did mean she missed out on some of the most important social aspects of school life. In contrast, other kids formed their little groups of friends quickly and easily and were soon hanging out together.

And although I tried to encourage her to socialise, and by now she had more of the necessary language tools to do so, it was heartbreaking that she had no hearing friends. I remember extending invitations to Sarah's classmates to come back to our house for tea after school, but these would typically be declined. At the same time, again she tended to be left out of invites to her classmates' birthday parties or to go round to theirs after lessons.

In particular, and like many children, Sarah found English and Maths especially tricky subjects. She once came back from school, for example, and we asked if she'd had a good day, she complained that she had found a poetry class especially hard because the poem had been written in 'old-fashioned English'! And sometimes, in her speaking and writing, she would tend to miss off the ends of words. So she was also developing her written communication skills at a slower rate than her peers.

Rather than full BSL lessons, Sarah only had Sign Supported English during her school years. (This is a kind of sign language which follows the structure of the English language as it is read and spoken.) Looking back now, we wonder about that and think that Sarah would probably have really benefited from a mix of both oral and signed lessons – so we think it would have been nice if she could have done both. But she would have had to have gone to a specialist deaf school for that.

Now, interestingly, she is really keen to brush up on her British Sign Language again, and we have been trying to find a suitable class near us so she can do that.

I'm sorry to say that sadly Sarah also experienced some pretty unpleasant bullying during her time in secondary school. There were a couple of other girls in particular, real class ringleaders, who would do low-level yet upsetting things like trying to trip her up when she was walking past, or pushing her. They were also verbally hurtful, calling her names and so on.

PE lessons would be a difficult time when they would be particularly spiteful to Sarah.

In my view, the school rather pushed the whole issue under the carpet and didn't act until it was too late. Each time I contacted them and got nowhere, I kept telling myself I had to give them more time to sort the problem out. But the hurtful name-calling and similar behaviour kept going on. Like many bullies, they were clever and did it in a way that meant they never got caught by the teachers, which was why it was able to persist for so long. It was relentless. But I was pleased that Sarah felt able to be open with me about what was happening, although, of course, it was horrible to see her so upset when she came home from school.

Eventually, however, the school did intervene and separated Sarah from the two ringleaders in class, and things gradually started to improve.

What we didn't know, even before Sarah had started at secondary school, was that a four-legged, furry-faced, waggy-tailed bundle of fun was about to come into our lives and change things significantly for the better.

ME AND WAFFLE

THE ARRIVAL OF WAFFLE IN OUR LIVES AND THE HUGE DIFFERENCE SHE MADE

Sarah was matched with her hearing dog Waffle in December 2012, when she was aged just nine and still in Year 5 at primary school.

We had decided to go for having a hearing dog after seeing something on the TV a year or two previously about how a dog could help someone in a situation like Sarah's – and she was really excited by the idea. We hadn't heard about assistance dogs before; like most people, we just had a vague idea about the notion of guide dogs for the blind. In our Muslim culture, most people don't keep dogs as pets, although they may own them as guard dogs. There certainly isn't a great tradition of walking the dog, which means that animals don't always get enough exercise.

With dogs being so close to the ground most of the time and people in our religion using the floor for praying, many have a belief that these animals are not clean. So one or two of my family members thought the idea of keeping one in our home was a bit odd! (Anyone who really thought that, however, would change their mind very quickly after meeting Waffle …)

But we were absolutely clear that this was what we wanted, no matter what anyone else thought. So when we got the email to say we had a match in a delightful white cockapoo called Waffle, we were all really buzzing. And because when we got Waffle it was just a few days before Christmas, it seemed to make the whole thing even more special. We could hardly have asked for a better present that year!

Waffle was born as part of the charity Hearing Dogs for Deaf People's breeding programme. At eight weeks of age, she went to a volunteer puppy socialiser for the next 18 months or so of her life. This was followed by six months' intensive work with a trainer at the charity's premises at The Grange in Buckinghamshire before she could become a certified hearing dog, and matched with a deaf human to go to her forever home.

Support from Hearing Dogs was excellent, and ongoing after we took Waffle home, with regular home visits and training and the charity regularly checked in with us all the time to see how we were doing. They really have been with us every single step of the way, and we can never thank them enough for that, or for Waffle.

Sarah always says that meeting Waffle was one of the happiest days of her life so far. The charity has family rooms, so we stayed at The Grange overnight, and the atmosphere was lovely as they were all about to break up for Christmas – and we even got to enjoy a festive lunch while we were there.

We were looking out of the window of the room and saw the trainer below, bringing Waffle to meet us for the first time. That was our first glimpse of the ball of fluff that would change our lives. All we could see was this gorgeous bundle of pale fur – and it was definitely love at first sight! That was a very special moment, and the bond between Sarah and her new best friend was instant. Instinctively, both seemed to know that it was the start of many adventures together, and that each one would change the other's life.

The charity works hard to match deaf people with hearing dogs whose temperaments suit each other. It became apparent very quickly just what an ideal match Sarah and Waffle were for one another. Waffle has a particularly gentle and sensitive nature, making her ideal to be placed with someone as young as Sarah and who, of course, faces a number of additional challenges. From their earliest time together, she instinctively seemed to know when Sarah seemed upset, and would offer comfort, for example by sitting in her lap or not leaving her side when she was sad.

That doesn't mean that Waffle can't sometimes be quite cheeky, though – for example when we take her little working jacket off and she shoots off chasing squirrels in the park on one of our daily walks. (In fact, this is one of the few times when she ever barks.) But she is never in a bad mood, and never conveys any feeling of not wanting to work. (Unlike some humans we can think of!)

Many people ask us what a hearing dog actually does. Put simply, Waffle acts as Sarah's ears. She alerts her to all the everyday sounds others take for granted, including the alarm clock, cooker timer, doorbell, phone and smoke alarms. If she ever thought Sarah may be in any danger, for example in the event of a fire, she would lie down flat on the floor.

Waffle can even carry little messages from the kitchen upstairs to Sarah, for example when dinner is ready and she wouldn't be able to hear if we called her down.

Waffle's ability to wake up Sarah and spend the night on her bed has made a huge difference to the peaceful daily life of our household. Previously, Sarah would regularly wake up in the night, just about every night, and come in to our room, which could get a little difficult since her dad, Majid, is a postman and so of course needs to be up early for work.

It also meant that Sarah would only fall in to a deep sleep in the early hours of the morning, so that inevitably she would be exhausted the next day, and we couldn't rouse her when it was time to get up for school. We tried changing the bed in her room, but nothing seemed to work. It was exhausting for all of us.

The problem with her sleep was understandable anxiety at being on her own in the dark and not being able to hear, but now that problem is eliminated, thanks to Waffle keeping her company.

Another important part of what a hearing dog does is to give a visible manifestation to an otherwise invisible disability. Waffle has a little burgundy jacket explaining she is a working assistance dog, which we put on her when we go out. Waffle's lead also has the charity's logo in highly visible colours, to make her more noticeable whenever we are out and about.

Interestingly, people don't always understand that deaf people can have assistance dogs – it's easy to assume only the blind have them. What's more, there can be an assumption that service or assistance animals are all Labradors, and that other breeds can't do the job. And certainly not everyone has heard of the Hearing Dogs for Deaf People charity.

That can mean that, just occasionally, we've experienced one or two access issues. A security guard at our local Sainsbury's insisted that Waffle wasn't allowed inside – he just couldn't seem to understand that she was a working assistance dog, and so perfectly allowed to enter the store with us. In the end, we had to speak to the store manager and thankfully the problem was soon sorted out, but it wasn't a particularly pleasant incident.

There was another issue once with the flagship M&S store in central London's Oxford Street, and then another time a security guard from our local shopping centre actually ran down the road after us! So we've had to quite a lot of educating about Waffle and why she is allowed to go anywhere we do.

Where Sarah is at college, Waffle can go in with her if she wants to, and she even has her own ID lanyard! But there have been cases over the years at school with Waffle not being allowed to go in to some school events when Sarah was younger, which has been frustrating. Whenever she is school or college, though, she quickly becomes the centre of attention. And she was always allowed in for Sarah's exams, which she would spend curled up under her desk, calming her owner's nerves just by being there with her.

We've never had as many conversations in public since Waffle came into our lives! Passers-by love to stop us and chat, and ask all about her; she's always the centre of attention.

Sarah says: "I'd never previously put myself in a situation where I would make eye contact or talk to someone I didn't know. I just wouldn't do it. I'd hope the person wouldn't speak to me. Mum tells the story of one birthday when I was younger (aged about eight) and we were in the queue at M&S, buying my birthday cake. A kindly woman just asked if the cake was for my birthday while we were waiting, and I just looked away. Mum had to explain to the lady that I was deaf.

"Another time, at a hospital appointment, Mum remembers that I wouldn't play with the toys and puzzles in the outpatients' department along with the other kids. Now she always says there's no shutting me up – and that she almost wishes I was as I was before!"

So Waffle has played an absolutely pivotal role in helping Sarah develop key social and communication skills and above all to build her confidence. She has enabled her to leave the house with her but no one human in tow, something her mum at one point thought may not be possible.

Because Sarah also plays a huge part in Waffle's care, including taking her for many of her daily walks and giving her food and water, grooming her and so on, dog ownership has also taught her a great deal about personal responsibility.

Finally, thanks to Waffle, Sarah has had so many adventures she would certainly never have otherwise have experienced, which we can't wait to tell you all about in the next chapter.

Sarah, Waffle and Sally, Waffles trainer. First time Sarah met Waffle. Picture taken at The Grange

first day Sarah met Waffle at the Grange

photo taken 6 months after matching with Waffle by Paul Wilkinson

first trip to seaside with Waffle .Bournemouth 2014

first Christmas with Waffle 2013

LEGOLAND *windsor 2014*

we did a bucket collection in aid of hearing dogs 2013

Sarah & Waffle

Sarah & Waffle playing in the snow. Waffle loves the snow

Waffle birthday

Great British Dog Walk in aid of Hearing dogs 2017

WAFFLE AND SARAH'S ADVENTURES TOGETHER

We think it is fair to say that when Waffle first came into our lives, we had no idea of just what lay ahead, or what we would go on to achieve together with her help, and we could never have even dreamt of all the adventures we've ended up having!

Here (and in no particular order – we adore looking back on all of them!) are the main things we've got up to over the years, apart, of course, from our participation in the world's most famous dog show Crufts, which we will look at in detail in the next chapter, since we reckon it merits a chapter of its own. And we have to say we've absolutely loved (and enjoyed something unique, different and special with) every single one of our adventures. We have to call them that, by the way, there is no other word that comes close to describing all the things we've done and achieved together.

- Our TrustedHousesitters.com green plaque

TrustedHousesitters is a global marketplace for the pet care and travel industries. Its Pet Plaques scheme is the first of its kind in the UK dedicated entirely to animals. The green circular metal plates (complete with pointy ears!) commemorate very special creatures, including living ones and those who are no longer with us. The plaques look similar to the English Heritage signs you often see denoting that someone famous once lived in a particular property.

At the time of writing, only 20 of the discs had even been awarded around the country, and each one is designed to take pride of place in the animal's home – with Waffle's being no exception in ours!

Nominations remain anonymous – so we will never be able to know who was kind enough to put our beloved Waffle forward, or be able to thank them. What's more, we reckon we'll probably never stop wondering who it was!

As the website for the company put it at the time: "More than just a family pet, Waffle the dog has become the 'ears' of his young owner, Sarah, who was born profoundly deaf. Their strong bond and unwavering friendship has given the 14-year-old confidence and helped her to reconnect with the world around her."

Sapedeh takes up the story: "The plaque reads: 'Home to the hearing dog who transformed her owner's life'. We couldn't have put it better ourselves! Waffle was the first hearing dog in the United Kingdom to receive one of these honours, and she was only the fifth ever animal to get a plaque. So we could not be prouder of Sarah or Waffle.

"We found out about this totally out of the blue, in a phone call somewhere near the start of 2019. I came off the phone in a bit of a daze, feeling shocked yet absolutely thrilled. Then the plaque itself arrived, maybe a month after that. We just felt so happy; it was surreal, really – in fact, it almost seemed too good to be true. We asked for the plaque to be posted to us – and we were all so happy and excited when it arrived!

"Of course, we were absolutely thrilled. And it has been nailed up outside the front door ever since. Visitors, from people we know well to the washing-machine repair man, often remark on it and we will always be pleased to take the time to explain the story. Again, it's another way of talking to people about Sarah's hidden disability and everything that Waffle does for her. So it's almost like an educational tool as well."

- The Rickshaw challenge

Since 2010, this charity staple has raised millions for the BBC's good cause Children in Need, the corporation's annual televised fundraising drive, with donations helping to transform so many young lives. The challenge essentially involves young people tackling routes UK-wide in a rickshaw each autumn, including from Edinburgh to Cambridge and Llandudno to Reading. The driving force behind it each year is the popular TV presenter Matt Baker.

In 2020, Sarah was over the moon to learn she was one of six children chosen to represent the hearing dogs charity as part of that year's project.

She says: "I was very excited at the thought of being pushed to my limits, and really loved the idea of leaving my comfort zone and doing something that I had never done before. Previously, I'd only ever cycled for a few minutes at a time. But I had come to realise that, with Waffle by my side, I could actually do just about anything!"

The seven-week training programme kicked off very soon after selection, and involved an hour and a quarter at a local cycle track ahead of the event, held at the Goodwood Estate, Sussex. (And it is a real challenge since it's certainly not a flat route!) There were regular Zoom meetings with organisers which we found helpful since they offered us a lot of encouragement. Of all the cyclists who took part that year, Sarah was the only one who was deaf.

It was agreed that, due to Covid restrictions in place at the time, the challenge would have to be held at the track rather than taking participants from town to town as was the case in previous years.

The cycling challenge was due to last five days, and it was going to replicate the same number of miles as previously. Unfortunately, after the first day, we took a call from organisers who rang us to say that, because a cameraman had tested positive for Covid, all the pedalling would now have to be completed at home.

Obviously, that came as a bit of a blow initially. But we very quickly adapted to the new set-up.

And that is exactly what Sarah did – she completed the whole challenge at home on an exercise bike – and Waffle was with her every step (or pedal!) of the way, even if she couldn't actually turn the pedals herself!

That year, BBC Children in Need raised £38m overall, the Rickshaw Challenge £5.8m, which was of course an incredible effort. Having been through a number challenges ourselves, we fully understand just how necessary the funds and support are. We're confident that money will change lives, just as our own lives have been changed.

There was another boost, too, when the TV supervet Noel Fitzpatrick spoke about hearing dogs on the BBC's *The One Show*, in reference to the rickshaw challenge, and he mentioned these assistance pets as a great example of the relationship between animals and humans working at its best. It's fair to say that we weren't expecting that at all, so (for once) we were pretty much shocked into speechlessness. But we were also, of course, thrilled to have someone like Noel Fitzpatrick offer his support via such a high-profile platform. So that left us feeling on a real high.

For Sarah in particular, as mentioned the only participant with a hearing dog, it's no exaggeration to say the rickshaw challenge was nothing short of life-changing. It has given her confidence and taught her even more determination, and to keep going even when things can feel tough. We are so grateful she had the opportunity to take part.

- Superhero Dogs Award 2021

Sarah and Waffle were nominated (once again, anonymously) for the 2021 Naturo SuperDog Awards – and, once again, to this day we still have no idea who put our names forward! But of course we were delighted, even if we weren't actually shortlisted on this occasion.

The awards, in the words of the organisers, 'recognise and celebrate the remarkable dogs who improve and enrich our lives'.

And it was so wonderful to read what they wrote about Sarah and Waffle on the website – they are words that sum up the relationship beautifully, so we'll always remember them:

"They are the best team ever, and Waffle is a hearing dog that has transformed her recipient's life."

- Play Your Pets Right

This was a BAFTA-winning TV series for Sky Kids which we were lucky enough to be chosen for, and loved taking part in. It is no longer aired on the telly, unfortunately, but Sarah and Waffle both loved doing this one so much. The show saw the nation's pets go head to head in fun-packed games which put owners and pets through their paces, and put the animals' speed, agility and focus to the test.

We filmed at a gorgeous country estate in truly wonderful grounds, with the lovely estate buildings and a red carpet in the background. We took part in this in 2019, before the lockdowns kicked in.

To explain it in a nutshell, the game saw Sarah standing at one end of the 'Tunnel of Temptation' encouraging Waffle on, with Sapedeh standing at the other end.

The tunnel was so-called because it was full of distracting canine treats for Waffle including toys and food. Waffle competed against one other dog in the race, and she came through the tunnel first, beating the other animal. We could not have been more proud of our girl!

We came away with a Play Your Pets Right ceramic bowl for Waffle to commemorate our participation in the show – not to mention many brilliant memories plus £100 in Amazon vouchers for Sarah.

So taking part was a really happy day, and yet another great adventure for Waffle and Sarah.

official photo Team Rickshaw 2020

play your pets right filming

filming for a TV program called play your pets right.

arrival of TrustedHousesitters Pet Plaques 2018, Waffle was commemorated

Sarah riding the Rickshaw along Matt Baker at Goodwood estate

pedaling at home, due to covid Team Rickshaw had to be done virtually at home

Waffle supporting Sarah, watching Sarah pedal for Rickshaw challenge

ALL THE FUN OF CRUFTS

It was first held in 1891, making it 130 years old, and it is the biggest event of its kind in the world. So it is hard to overstate the significance of Crufts, the international dog show held every year at the NEC in Birmingham and organised by the UK's Kennel Club. It attracts attendees from all over the world. And if you'd have told us that we'd be involved in this prestigious event with Waffle when we first got her, we'd simply never have believed you!

At Crufts, there are essentially a number of competitions going on at the same time. And while the most important contest that everyone has heard of is the Best in Show award, there are plenty of other competitions in everything from obedience to agility and even heelwork to music.

Then there is also the prestigious Friends for Life category, which is held at Crufts each year to celebrate the nation's unsung canine heroes.

For us, the Crufts experience was back in 2018, and Sarah and Waffle were nominated by a friend of ours, who also happened to be called Sarah. She is a fellow dog lover and also enters animals herself into shows like Crufts all the time.

We knew we'd been nominated for Crufts, and of course, were thrilled, but, to be honest, we promptly forgot all about it! But Sarah had put us forward for a new category of the show's Friends for Life section, called Child's Hero.

Then we got a phone call out of the blue, a few months after the initial nomination, explaining that they were taking things a stage further. As mentioned, we had completely forgotten all about Crufts. But we were so excited and we genuinely couldn't believe the news. There may even have been some shouting!

Over the telephone, we excitedly arranged a time and date for someone from Crufts to come to the house to do an interview with us. And one of the hardest things was that we had to keep the whole thing to ourselves. We weren't allowed to tell anyone outside the three of us until the broadcast had gone out via the show's current national broadcaster, Channel 4. That was so hard, as we're naturally chatty and highly sociable people, and we're so proud of Sarah and Waffle and all they've achieved together that we can't help but want to share all their successes with everyone.

The team from Crufts turned up with a heap of camera equipment and stayed with us for several hours, interviewing both Sapedeh and Sarah. We were also filmed taking Waffle for a walk locally and so on, and the resulting video went online on the show's website.

The next step was that we had to travel up to the headquarters of the Kennel Club in London shortly afterwards, and here we met the other finalists. There was also an exciting photo shoot in the city's beautiful Hyde Park, which we really loved doing; it was such a pleasure.

The following day, the club told us the results of the votes, made by members of the public on social media. And the hearing dogs charity had also really promoted us on its own social channels. (But we'll keep you dangling a little while longer before telling you what they were …)

Among the other finalists that year were a rescue border collie, a search and rescue dog and a disabled canine partner. We all ended up spending so much time together that we have become good friends who remain in touch with each other and love hearing each other's news.

We first heard about the nomination being taken forward in January 2018. Then in March, we stayed in Birmingham for Crufts weekend. That was a huge experience, not least because we really didn't know much about the show beforehand. And we'd certainly never been to it previously, or even seen it on TV. So we had no idea just how exciting it would all be.

Equally, we really loved the way it showcased what hearing dogs can do, and how they can completely change lives, in such a public forum. After all, there are thousands of seats in that arena, with 160,000 in attendance the year we were there, not to mention a huge TV audience, and it always surprises us how few people really understand about dogs like Waffle and what they can do.

Without a doubt, the most exciting part of the whole weekend was doing the lap of honour in front of everyone on Sunday afternoon. The applause was incredible – it was totally deafening!

Sarah says: "Of course, I felt nervous before going on national television, as anyone would be if they had never done it before. I explained to everyone that Waffle is my best friend. I was anxious at first but keen to explain how important she is to me, so once I was out there, I just gave it everything I had."

Sapedeh says: "From a child who could not make eye contact with anyone, to a teenager who is capable of doing something like this – the transformation has been just unbelievable."

The occasion was made even more exciting because the former Spice Girl and all-round pop superstar, Geri Horner (AKA Ginger Spice) was presenting it. We're now huge fans of hers! She was lovely, actually. And there was intense interest in her at the time, as rumours were swirling that weekend of a possible Spice Girls reunion, leading to even more and higher-profile coverage in the national press than the event might otherwise have received.

However, as it turned out, in the end, we didn't win our category. That honour went to an adorable pooch called Jack and his owner Vanessa, and it was so very well deserved, so of course, there were no hard feelings. But we will never forget everything that taking part in Crufts did for us – it was one more adventure to notch up with Waffle, one we could never, ever have imagined happening before she came into our lives and turned everything upside down.

Official photo taken at Hyde Park for Friends for Life at Crufts, 2018

back stage photo , when friends for life 2018 finalist was announced official photo released by kennel club taken at hide park .friends for life finalist 2018

Sarah & Waffle at Hyde park, for friends for life 2018 photo shoot

Sarah & Waffle getting ready to go in main arena for the winner of Friends for life 2018 to be announced

photo by Nicky Stock

Sarah & Waffle, Sarah wearing her rosette Crufts Friends for life finalist 2018

LOOKING FORWARD TO THE FUTURE WITH CONFIDENCE

We have come across a variety of attitudes towards Waffle over all the years that we have had her. At Uxbridge College, she now even has her own lanyard and ID card, and we explained how important she is to us when we attended the open day, so Sarah can take her in whenever she wants to. And people even ask where she is if she is not around because her little furry face is so familiar to them! But that does not mean that everything has always been plain sailing.

We've mentioned previously about Waffle being denied access to some shops on a few occasions. But sometimes we even ran into problems at school, as well, which is perhaps the last place you'd expect to run into difficulties when trying to accommodate a child's special needs.

When Sarah was in Years 7 through 9, for example, disappointingly the school wasn't happy at all with having a dog on the premises, and they claimed they were worried about children who might have allergies. During her primary school years, we even had to keep Waffle away from special events such as sports days which were held outside. Whenever Waffle has been around, though, she has very quickly become the centre of attention!

As Sarah says: "My classmates love her nearly as much as I do! So it is always a shame and surprise to come up against negative attitudes towards my best friend. I actually find it quite hurtful."

Sarah was particularly keen to have Waffle with her at times of heightened anxiety, such as on the days when she would be sitting exams. (With these, she would simply curl up under Sarah's desk, calming her nerves just by being there.) And it was after around Christmas that she was in Year 10, in secondary school, when things did at long last get a bit easier, and from then on she was indeed allowed to have Waffle with her on exam days.

Waffle also provided a lot of reassurance when Sarah started playing table tennis in the London Borough of Hillingdon's schools competition. This is yet another great achievement of hers, and in fact she was the first deaf girl to take part in this event. By now, of course, she has broken down so many barriers that we are almost used to it!

Sarah is now on the point of turning 19 and, as it is for any young woman of that age, it's a time when thoughts are starting to turn to the future and wondering what that might look like. But the time has also come for us to start thinking about having another hearing dog.

Sarah explains: "Waffle makes me feel as though I can do anything I want. I am so excited about whatever lies ahead and feel that I have a lot to look forward to and a great future. I understand that I have some way to go, for example with my organisational skills and other things. But I also know that I can face the future with confidence, maybe even, with the right support, living independently in my own place at some point. No one thought I'd ever be able to do that before. Everything will always be easier and far more achievable with either Waffle or another dog constantly at my side."

Sapedeh adds: "Sarah has changed quite a lot in recent years, as any young girl growing up would, and has come such a very long way. She takes Waffle out and about by herself all the time, for example, and I never thought she would be able to do that. And it's all because of her best friend completely transforming her life."

Waffle has also introduced us to many other people who we would not have otherwise met. At The Grange in Buckinghamshire where they train hearing dogs, for example, they have annual community days where they introduce you to other beneficiaries and their hearing dogs. Here, we have met and got to know some amazing people who volunteer for the charity and who put their free time and effort into socialising puppies and getting them ready for their sound work training, so that one day they can go on to change a deaf person's life, just as Waffle has changed Sarah's.

It was also at The Grange that we met Polly, a year or so younger than Sarah, and her labrador, Kass. The dogs and girls got on very well with each other! So it's always great when we can catch up with them.

Sarah has now grown into a confident young woman, thanks to Waffle's help. At the time we wrote this book, she was looking forward to finishing her two-year media course at college, and gaining her NVQ Level 3, which gives young people the potential to go on to study at university. Again, this isn't something we could ever have imagined pre-Waffle.

She loves making videos in particular and has become a talented young filmmaker, and so she would love to take this skill further as part of a Media Studies degree – and even dreams of working for the BBC and making programmes for them.

But wherever Sarah's life takes her, her future is bound always to have a hearing dog at the heart of it. However, we're also very aware that nothing can stay the same forever …

With hearing dogs, smaller breeds are retired at 11 or 12 years of age, while bigger ones retire when they are about ten years old, as it is around that age that they can start to develop some health issues. That means that, from around November 2022, Waffle will need to retire, and Sarah is on the waiting list to be matched with a successor hearing dog. Of course, we know that Waffle can never truly be replaced. Ever. But, inevitably, we also know she can't go on forever. She will need to rest and let another hearing dog do all the work for a change! Obviously, she won't be going anywhere away from us. She and Sarah will always remain the closest of buddies, and Waffle will still be here as a much-loved family pet and will be here for Sarah, as she always has been. After all, she has been with Sarah since she was nine and has seen her grow up from a child into a young woman. And she knows instinctively when she is upset, so she's been there through all the emotional challenges of growing up. She'll instinctively jump in her lap to offer comfort. No one ever wants that to change.

So, undoubtedly, Waffle is a very hard act to follow indeed. She has the sweetest nature, never losing her temper or barking aggressively at anyone, no matter what happens. She will always play happily with other dogs in the park and she has always been so sociable and friendly, as well as extremely gentle.

But she's already, unfortunately, had a few health scares in recent years, which has made us realise that she won't be able to work with Sarah forever. But although she is starting to struggle a little bit now, that certainly doesn't affect her ability to do her job, and Waffle continues to do really well. She and Sarah are still very much a team.

But, a few years ago, our beloved Waffle needed an operation for her leg on what is called a cruciate ligament, and we needed to put her on what were told is a satiety diet to keep her weight low. The cruciate ligaments are the two strips of fibrous tissue in each knee. They connect the bones above and below the knee joint to keep it hinged and stable.

That was a tough one to go through, as we hate denying her anything, but we were able to substitute Waffle's regular treats with carrot-based ones. Not only does she love these just as much as the ones we used to give her, but they are also a whole lot healthier.

And, on top of that, Waffle lost an eye due to a tumour, in February 2021. She was blinking so much that we knew something was troubling her, so we took her straight to see an emergency vet. They told us that she just had an eye infection, but for some reason, we weren't completely convinced, so we took her to an animal hospital which specialises in treating dogs, about an hour and 15 minutes drive from where we live. They kept Waffle in overnight to monitor the pressure on her eye.

It was a pretty stressful time for all of us, so certainly not one we will forget in a hurry; in fact, it was so scary because we weren't even entirely sure whether Waffle would even be coming home. So we kept in touch with the welfare team at the hearing dogs charity throughout. It turned out that Waffle needed treatment from an eye specialist at a different veterinary hospital about 20 minutes from the other one.

We had to wait anxiously at home rather than at the hospital while Waffle had her left eye removed, due to the Covid restrictions which were in place at the time. However, you can imagine our relief when we were told that the op had been a complete success and that we could go and pick our best friend up and bring her home where she belonged again.

And we have to say we are very proud of the way she has adapted so quickly to having just one eye. She has just gotten used to it, and it doesn't seem to bother her at all. But then, Waffle is so amazing that it's hardly surprising.

But we have had to come to accept that Sarah will need a new working dog in due course. Sarah is on the waiting list waiting to be matched with a successor dog. Of course, there is likely to be a period of adjustment, but we know Waffle will welcome her successor as much as we will, and we're pleased that she'll have a chance to get the rest she needs.

But, as mentioned, Waffle remains and will remain at the heart of our family life – and it is really hard to imagine life without her. No one can ever know exactly what the future holds for any of us. But we do know we, and Sarah in particular can face it with a great deal more confidence thanks to a certain adorable, furry, four-legged friend of ours!

Who would have thought that that lovable furball we met all those years ago, when Sarah was still a very young schoolgirl, could have had such a powerful and lasting impact on all our lives?

ME AND WAFFLE

MORE ABOUT HEARING DOGS

Hearing dogs like Waffle are highly trained to alert deaf people to important and potentially life-saving sounds that they might otherwise not hear. These include everything from a smoke alarm to the doorbell and even a crying baby in need of attention. If a deaf person can be made aware of such things, it can completely change their lives, including their ability to live fully independently. So it's important to remember that these are hard-working assistance dogs and that they're most definitely not pets.

However, these clever canines do so much more than alerting their human to the various noises which they need to hear. Just as vital are the companionship and affection these animals supply in endless quantities! Unless you have a hearing loss yourself, you may not realise just how lonely and isolating living with deafness can be. But, thanks to hearing dogs, their owners can reconnect with their life and live it to the full.

The charity that trains and matches them with humans, Hearing Dogs for Deaf People, which has already helped thousands of deaf people, was first launched 40 years ago, back in 1982, and has more than 1,100 active working hearing dog partnerships across the UK. Training and supporting each one costs in the region of £40,000 over an animal's lifetime.

Hearing Dogs may have been initially launched at Crufts, but its origins are far more humble. In fact, its original home was the living room of founder member Gill Lacey, who at the time had a mere three members of staff. In 1983, the UK's first ever hearing dog, Lady, was matched with her deaf human and history was made. Hearing Dogs has grown steadily in size every year ever since.

It gained official charitable status in 1986, and the Princess Royal, Princess Anne, has been its patron for some three decades.

By 1990, less than 10 years after it was founded, the charity had doubled in size and had already placed its hundredth dog, Spring, during this year. (By 2004, the thousandth dog, Ria, had been matched with her deaf human.)

In 2006, a 10-year-old girl named Chloe became the first child to benefit from a partnership with a hearing dog – and the dog was even trained to pass notes between the girl and her older brother!

Today the charity runs thanks in no small part due to the efforts of an army of 3,000 volunteers, and there is a training centres in Yorkshire as well as in Buckinghamshire.

The journey to partnership: how hearing dogs are trained

- The first eight weeks: Puppies remain with their mum during this time, and typically live in the home of a volunteer.
- Next steps: A puppy arrives at The Grange centre in Buckinghamshire at around eight weeks of age to kick off their training. They move through a series of three 'stars' as they learn more about the world around them, good behaviour and social interactions before gaining more responsibility as they learn to make decisions. Training is complex and varied, as

you can probably imagine, involving socialising, distraction, obedience and sound training. It's also reward-based, meaning bad or unwanted behaviour goes ignored, while good behaviour is acknowledged with a favourite toy or a treat, or a big fuss is made about the hearing dog in training.

The charity says: "Our pups become part of the family. And, as they mature, they learn crucial sound work and alerts that allow them to help their future deaf partner. At around the age of 14 to 16 months, a pup is typically ready to move to 'big school' and begin their 'sound work' – or advanced training."

- Final matching and training: After passing the first three puppy stars, the next stage is advanced training and meeting the deaf person with whom they will be placed. The fourth star is about fine-tuning their training so that they're all ready for their final assessment.

The matching process, completed during the final stages of training, is done with a great deal of care and attention. It takes expert knowledge to create a 'perfect fit' with the right deaf person and their needs and individual personality. For example, an energetic Labrador wouldn't be the perfect companion for someone frail; but they could ideally suit someone sporty who is very active and always out running or walking.

Before the organisation can match a dog to their deaf human, so many things have to be taken into account. These include, for example, whether someone's home is in a city or a small village, whether they have other pets a hearing dog would need to become acquainted with, their individual needs, their social, family and working lives, how active they are, and many other factors to boot.

The charity carefully assesses each dog's personal strengths, likes and dislikes and so on. In this way, it can create the perfect pairing between canine and human.

Once a match is found and human and dog are introduced, things can move pretty quickly if they get along with each other. A pre-placement week takes place at The Grange or The Beatrice Wright Centre, the sister centre in Yorkshire, or at the deaf person's home.

It is at this point that training ends, and the bond between human and canine is truly forged and the life of the partnership begins.

Breeding hearing dogs

Hearing dogs work with three breeds plus a single cross-breed – poodles, cocker spaniels and labradors – and cockapoos.

Volunteer foster carers are enlisted to look after the hearing dogs chosen for the breeding scheme. Selected mums will give birth to three to four litters before they retire.

How Sapedeh became involved as a volunteer
Sapedeh says:
Just six months after Sarah and Waffle were matched, I decided to put myself forward and registered as a volunteer for Hearing Dogs for Deaf People. I could see for myself not

only the incredible difference Waffle had made to Sarah's life, but the impact she had on us a family at the same time.

These dogs help deaf people to combat loneliness, and to reconnect more fully with life. And the charity also gives help, advice and support to anyone living with a hearing loss. So while hearing dogs are for those with severe hearing difficulty, the charity also operates Hearing Link, offering a help desk, self-help and rehab courses as well as support groups. It does such a lot.

I've now volunteered for the organisation for about nine years, and it has been so wonderful seeing so many people give their time to the charity so freely and to see how committed they all are. They are with the dogs every step of the way, from the moment they are born to the moment they are matched with their recipient and beyond. So it's a lifelong commitment, really.

Indeed, the volunteers are the beating heart of the organisation, and so it's no wonder I have so much respect for them! It is they, really, who make the partnerships happen.

So during my journey, I have something I never thought I would gain – a second family, and one I am extremely proud to have met and to be part of, our Team Burgundy family! (So called because of the liveried jackets in this colour that the dogs wear.)

I go out on bucket collections, speak anywhere I can about hearing dogs, at any event where someone is needed to represent the charity. And it is something I really enjoy doing. It even makes me forget about all my own stresses and worries.

I never tire of explaining the benefits of having a hearing dog, from the practical benefits of hearing anything from the doorbell to the morning alarm clock to the way a canine companion helps build confidence. And how taking them out for daily walks helps forge new friendships with humans as well.

Because the dog goes everywhere with their deaf partners, they feel increasingly able to go out, socialise and try new things. We know that feelings of isolation and loneliness are common among those with a hearing loss. A working dog can definitely put an end to those feelings, as we have seen happen ourselves with Sarah.

For a couple of hours, we not only spread the word about hearing dogs, but we all come together for the same reason – because this cause is so very close to our hearts.

I'm also really fortunate to have had the chance to go out and see some of the organisation's puppies at first hand, very shortly after they have been born, and before they go to be with a socialiser when they are around eight weeks of age. Too cute!

So, in short, Waffle has done far more than just provide Sarah with a pair of charmingly fluffy ears. She has also given us a second family – our lovely Team Burgundy! She really is the gift that just keeps on giving.

Hearing Dogs for Deaf People in numbers

- Around 200 employees
- More than 3,300 volunteers
- Over 1,000 dogs with deaf partners

- Helps around 5,000 people annually
- In any one year, the charity will train dozens of puppies

Waffle in her Hearing Dog bandana

on train, Waffle in her Hearing Dog uniform

Waffle at 8 weeks old

SARAH AND SAPEDEH IN THEIR OWN WORDS

If you have a broken leg or use a wheelchair, other people are obviously able to see it. A blind person often has a white stick as well as a guide dog, making their condition highly visible. But what many people tend to forget is that deafness is very much a hidden disability. Because it has its own language, it also has its own culture, in a way that sight loss doesn't. And it's interesting because if you speak to someone with a hearing loss, it affects the other person as well as the deaf one. There can be frustration, or either a complete lack of or poor communication, in a way that doesn't happen if you are blind. So it's something that's a unique issue.

I had my first cochlear implant when I was just three years old, the second when I was a year older than that. I was so small that obviously I can't really remember life without them, or having them fitted. Since then, I've undergone 15 years of speech and language therapy. The implants have meant that I have had to relearn each individual sound, as if from new.

My mum remembers that when my implant was finally switched on (a long three months after surgery!) and I heard sounds, but could not recognise what they were. That's why I've needed to have speech therapy to support me throughout all the years which have gone by since then.

However, when I go to bed at night, and I take my implants out, I am completely deaf and can't hear a thing. When I have a shower, go swimming, or it's raining, I obviously also need to be sure I remove them then, as well, since they will stop working if they come into prolonged contact with more than a few drops of water.

Since the age of two, I have been heavily reliant on lip-reading. And even when I do have my implants on my head and switched on, I still struggle to hear and rely a lot on seeing people's faces and mouths, especially in a busy environment.

In fact, I spend so much time concentrating on what people are saying to me throughout the day that when I get home from college, I can feel completely exhausted. I like to take my implants off for an hour or so at this point in the day, allowing me just to relax in complete silence to ease this fatigue a little.

It's particularly hard on days when I have a conversation with someone but they don't make eye contact and don't even face me when they're talking to me. It's really difficult when I can't see their lips – I just have to take a guess at what they are trying to tell me. Or I'll keep saying "Sorry, can you please repeat what you have just said?"

When Covid hit and everyone was forced to wear a facemask, inevitably I found that especially challenging, as indeed many people with a hearing loss did, all over the world.

It meant I had no idea at all what people were saying to me. There was one point when I felt I could not face leaving the house at all – even though, of course, we were in lockdown for huge chunks of the pandemic.

I was so embarrassed because I was scared that people would think I was rude if I ignored them. My levels of anxiety went through the roof. Covid was really hard for everyone but I found it especially hard – although, of course, we all came out the other side.

So it certainly hasn't all been plain sailing. My mum Sapedeh takes up the story from an incident, going back a few years now, which is a good example of the various challenges we continue to face:

"In September 2014, about eight years ago at the time of writing, Sarah went to bed as normal in the evening. In the morning when I went to get her up and ready for school, I noticed some discharge on Sarah's pillow. At first, I thought it had come from her ear canal. I checked and it wasn't, so I lifted Sarah's hair and saw that the puss was coming from the inner coil beneath the skin on Sarah's skull.

"I then saw that the skin was broken, forming a hole forming the exact shape of where the inner coil sits on the skull. I knew immediately that this was very serious, and needed immediate action.

"I made a couple of urgent calls to the cochlear team at UCLH explaining what I had seen. I was advised to bring my daughter in immediately, so we set off for London straight away. When we got there, Sarah's cochlear implant consultant was already waiting for us.

"As soon as we arrived, they called us into a room where there were three other consultants waiting. That was when I understood that there was something pretty wrong going on. They checked Sarah, before the consultant explained that the internal part of Sarah's implant had become infected and that the infection had burst out through the skin.

"He then explained that the right-hand implant needed to be explanted as soon as possible since it was causing the skin to rupture even more. Sarah was rushed to the theatre right away so that this could happen.

"Once the operation was finished and she was on the ward she was put on an intravenous drip and had to remain in the hospital for the next five days. The staff there was amazing. I stayed with Sarah on the ward, while her dad came and visited us every day during visiting hours. Majid brought Waffle with him every time, and actually, it was then and only then that Sarah had a smile on her face. Those hours with Waffle were so precious since they were the only occasions she was really able to forget she was in the hospital.

"So it's been a real roller-coaster of emotions for all of us, as mentioned before. As parents, we have often felt so helpless at not being able to do more. Obviously, the operation and the dramatic dash to the hospital were a huge shock and worry for everyone involved.

"But thankfully Sarah was discharged from the hospital five days after being admitted. The consultant and cochlear implant team did tell us she would need to wait between six and seven months to have a replacement implant fitted back onto that side of her head. It meant that Sarah had to get used to coping with just a single implant. Understandably and inevitably, she really struggled to make much sense of the world without them until the day she was able to have her right ear implanted once again.

"The team kept a close eye on her progress. The site healed nicely, although in the end, it took nine full months before she was able to have implant surgery again for that ear. As ever, Waffle was by Sarah's side 24/7, helping ease the emotional and mental strain of some very difficult months.

"It was June 2015 by the time we got the call for Sarah to be fitted with a second right-hand cochlear implant. Just two weeks later, she was undergoing the surgery. It did mean she needed to go through speech and language therapy once again, even though she had previously had the same ear implanted. But, as always she just got on with it.

"Understandably, she has been through so much with her implants that she had got to a point now she can be wary of them on both sides of her head, and we know she worries that something could go wrong again.

"But the really brilliant news is that, since then, she simply has never looked back. What a journey our Sarah has been on. Her determination has taught Majid and me so much. It has been wonderful seeing our girl blossom into such a strong-minded young woman, despite all the various barriers and obstacles life has thrown at her.

"Whatever has happened, Sarah has just shined through and come out the other side stronger, time after time. We could not be more proud of our daughter – and have no doubt that she will go on to achieve whatever she wants in life.

"And as for Waffle, we just wish we could thank her for all she has done for Sarah and the family. But, somehow, we think she does know what she means to us all."

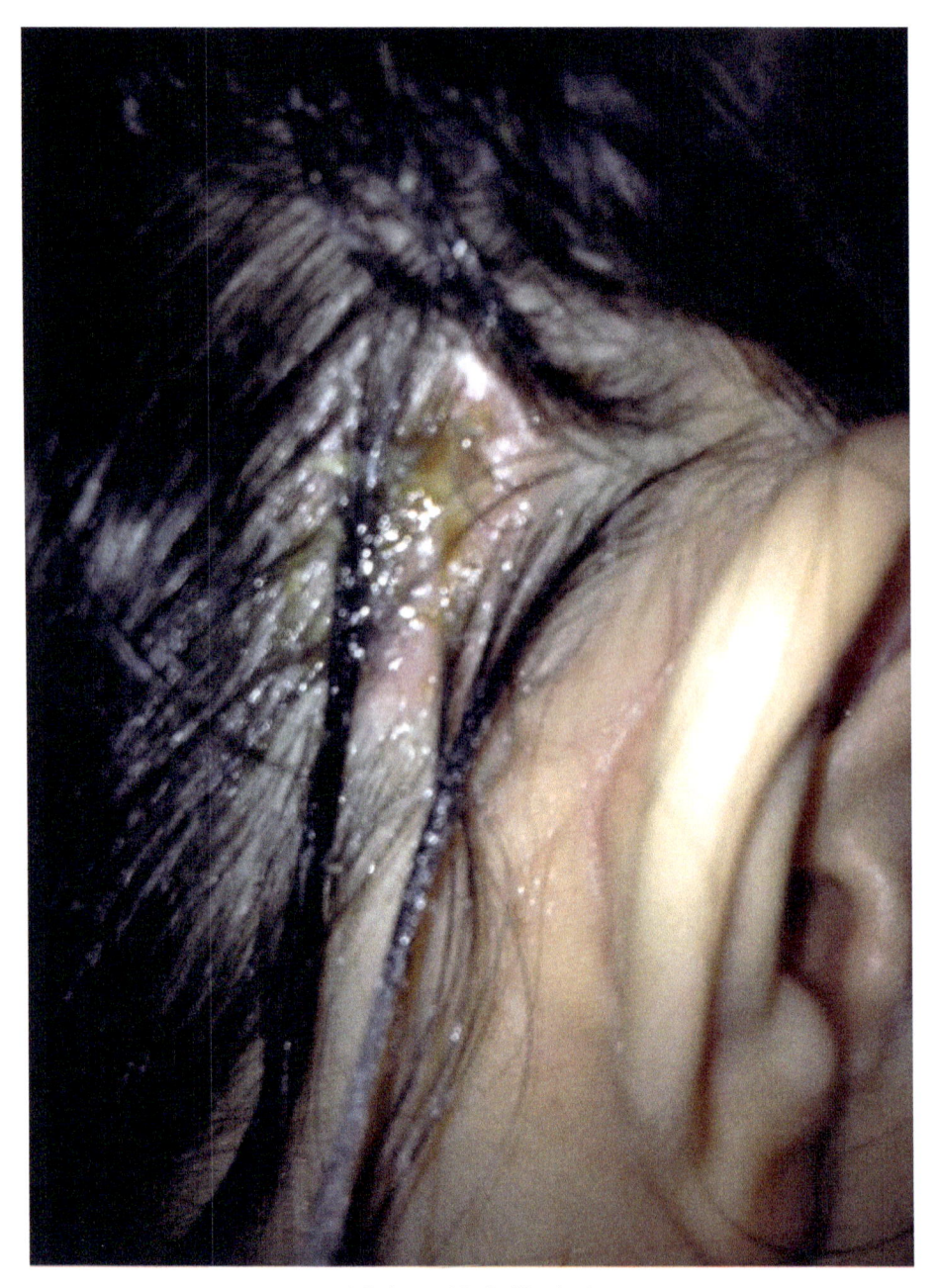

infection on right Cochlear implant

StoryTerrace

Printed in Great Britain
by Amazon